THE DESTRUCTION OF
JERUSALEM

An Absolute and Irresistible Proof of the Divine
Origin of Christianity:

ILLUSTRATED EDITION

INCLUDING A NARRATIVE OF
THE CALAMITIES WHICH BEFEL THE JEWS
So far as they tend to verify
OUR LORD'S PREDICTIONS
Relative to that event.

George Peter Holford

Charleston, AR:

COBB PUBLISHING

2021

Published in the United States of America by:
Cobb Publishing
704 E. Main St.
Charleston, AR 72933
CobbPublishing@gmail.com
CobbPublishing.com
479.747.8372

ISBN: 978-1-947622-70-8

Contents

PREFACE

History records few events more interesting than the destruction of Jerusalem and the Jewish state by the arms of the Romans. The intimate connection with the dissolution of the Levitical system, and the establishment of Christianity in the world; the striking verification of so many of the prophecies, both of the Old and New Testament, and the powerful arguments of the divine authority of the Scriptures which are thence derived; the solemn warnings and admonitions which they hold out to all nations, but especially such as are favored with the light and blessings of revelation; together with the impressive and terrific grandeur of the events themselves — are circumstances which must always insure this subject demands more than ordinary degrees of interest and importance. Many eminent and learned men have employed their pens in the illustration of it; but the fruits of their labors are, for the most part, contained in large and expensive works, out of the reach of numbers, to whom the discussion might prove equally interesting and instructive.

For the sake of these, the present treatise, in a more accessible and familiar form, is diffidently offered to the public. In order that it might be better adapted for the general reader, critical inquiries and tedious details are equally avoided; but it has been the care of the writer not to omit any important fact or argument that, in his opinion, tended to illuminate the subject. Countenanced by the example of many respectable names, he has ventured to introduce the extraordinary *phenomena*, which, according to Josephus, preceded the destruction of the *Holy City*. He has also added a few sentences in their defense, but he does not intend thereby to express his unqualified admission of their genuineness.

Usefulness is the writer's main object; and if a perusal of it shall contribute, under the Divine Blessing, to confirm the wavering faith of only one *Christian*, or to shake the vain confidence of a single *Unbeliever*, his labor will be abundantly rewarded.

G. H., London, 1805..

Jesus was a Prophet

The goodness of God stamps all His proceedings. It has pleased Him not only to communicate a revelation, which, to the pious mind, bears in its *internal* texture its own evidence and recommendation, but also to accompany it with such *external* proofs of a sacred origin, as seem calculated to strike with irresistible conviction, even those who are least disposed to admit the truth of the Holy Scriptures. In order to evidence their divine authenticity, God has done as much as man could possibly have required.[1] For, supposing that man could have selected the credentials which His messengers should bring with them, in order to authenticate the divinity of their mission--could the wisest and most skeptical amongst men have proposed, for this purpose, anything more conclusive than,

1. Demonstrations of power, surpassing every possible effect of human skill and effort — and
2. Intelligence relative to future events and circumstances of nations and individuals, which no human sagacity would ever pretend to foresee or predict?

If such had been the evidences demanded, what addition to them could possibly have been suggested? Is it in the human mind to imagine any tests of divine authority better adapted, sooner or later, to expose the artifices, and frustrate

---

[1] This assertion is sufficient for the writer's purpose. — The fact, however, is that the Almighty has, in this respect (as well as in every other) done for man "exceeding abundantly above" that which he can *ask* or *think*. — The scheme of that evidence which demonstrates the divine authority of the Bible could only have been constructed by Him "who knows all things," and who sees the end from the beginning.

the designs of an imposter? In vain will the profoundest policy attempt to discover means more suitable to this purpose, and, with respect to the reception of the revelation itself, more perfectly fitted to banish all reasonable doubt on the one hand, and to invalidate the charge of credulity on the other. Now these, precisely, *are* the credentials with which it has pleased God to sanction the testimony of His inspired messengers, as recorded in the Scriptures of the Old and New Testament.

THEY WROUGHT MIRACLES
THEY FORETOLD FUTURE EVENTS.

Thus all that man himself could demand has been given, and objectors are left entirely without excuse.

JESUS CHRIST, the principal of those messengers, like His illustrious types and predecessors, Moses and Elijah, proclaimed and attested His divine mission at once by miraculous acts and prophetic declarations.

His miracles were numerous, diversified, and performed in various parts of his native country. They were not frivolous tricks, calculated merely to excite wonder and gratify curiosity, but acts of substantial utility and benevolence. They were publicly, but not boastingly and ostentatiously, displayed — in the presence not of friends only, but also of enemies — of enemies exasperated to malignity against Him, because He had censured their vices and exposed their hypocrisy, and who were actuated by every motive which a spirit of revenge could suggest to incurable prejudice, to induce them to detect the imposition of His miracles, if *false*, and to deny and discredit them, if *true*. To *deny* them they did not attempt, but they strove to sink them in disrepute, and thereby furnished a striking specimen of those embarrassing dilemmas, into which infidelity is continually betraying her votaries. They ascribed them to the agency of Satan; thus representing Him, "who was a liar from the beginning," as contributing to the diffusion of the truth — "the spirit that works in the children of disobedience" as promoting the cause of holiness and as cooperating in the *overthrow of his own kingdom*, with HIM who "was manifested to *destroy* the works of the Devil!!!"

The prophecies of our Lord, as well as His miracles, were many, and of great variety. They were not delivered with pomp and parade, but rose out of occasions, and seem to have resulted, for the most part, from His affectionate solicitude for those who then were, or might afterwards become, His disciples. While the fulfillment of some of these predictions was confined to the term of his mission and the limits of his country, the accomplishment of others extended to all nations, and to every future age of the world.

FALL OF JERUSALEM.

A Description of Jerusalem in Jesus' Time

Of the prophecies which have already been fulfilled, few are so interesting or so striking in their accomplishment, as those which relate to the *destruction of Jerusalem and its Temple*, and the signal calamities which everywhere befell the Jewish nation. The *chief* of our Lord's predictions, relative to these events, are contained in Matthew 24, Mark 13, and Luke 21, and we may with confidence appeal to the *facts* which verify them as conclusive and incontrovertible proofs of the divinity of his mission. Before, however, we enter upon this illustration, it may be gratifying to the reader, and add considerably to the interest of many of the subsequent pages, to give in this place a brief description of that renowned city and its temple.

Jerusalem was built on two mountains. Three sets of celebrated walls surrounded the city on every side, except that which was deemed inaccessible, and there it was defended by one wall only. The most ancient of these walls was remarkable for its great strength, and was, moreover, erected on a hanging rock, and fortified by sixty towers. On the middle wall there were fourteen towers only; but on the third, which was also distinguished by the extraordinary merit of its architecture, there were no less than ninety. The celebrated tower of Psephinos, before which Titus (the Roman general) at first encamped, was erected on this latter wall, and even excelled it in the superior style of its architecture: it was seventy cubits [105 feet] high and had eight angles, each of which commanded most extensive and beautiful prospects. In clear weather, the spectator had from them a view of the Mediterranean Sea, of Arabia, and of the whole extent of the Jewish dominions. Besides this there were three other towers of great magnitude, named Hippocos, Phasael, and Mariamne. The two former, famed for their strength and grandeur, were nearly ninety cubits [135 feet] high; the latter, for its valuable curiosities, beauty, and elegance, was about fifty-five cubits [83 feet]. They were all built of white marble; and so exquisite was the workmanship, that each of them appeared as if it had been hewn out of an immense single block of it. Notwithstanding their great elevation, they yet must have appeared, from the surrounding country, far loftier than they really were. The old wall, it has just been remarked, was built upon a high rock: but these towers were erected upon the *top* of a hill, the summit of which was itself thirty cubits [45 feet] above the *top* of the old wall! Such edifices, so situated, it is easy to conceive, must have given to the city a very great degree of grandeur and magnificence.

Not far distant from these towers stood the royal palace, of singular beauty and elegance. Its pillars, its porticoes, its galleries, its apartments, were all incredibly costly, splendid, and superb; while the groves, gardens, walks, fountains, and aqueducts with which it was encompassed, formed the richest and most delightful scenery that can possibly be imagined. The situation of these structures was on the north side of Jerusalem.

Its celebrated temple, and the strong fort of Antonia, were on the east side, and directly opposite to the Mount of Olives. This fort was built on a rock fifty cubits [75 feet] in height, and so steep as to be inaccessible on every side; and to render it still more so, it was faced with thin slabs of marble, which, being slippery, proved at once a defense and an ornament. In the midst of the fort stood the *castle* of Antonia, the interior parts of which, for grandeur, state, and convenience, resembled more a palace than a fortress. Viewed from a distance it had the appearance of a tower, encompassed by four other towers, situated at the four angles of a square. Of these latter, three were fifty cubits [75 feet] high, and the fourth seventy cubits [135 feet].

The tower last mentioned commanded an excellent view of the whole temple, the riches, grandeur, and elegance of which it is not in the power of language to describe. Whether we consider its architecture, its dimensions, its magnificence, its splendor, or the sacred purposes to which it was dedicated, it must equally be regarded as the most astonishing fabric that was ever constructed. It was erected partly on a solid rock, which was originally steep on every side. The foundations of what was called the lower temple were 300 cubits [450 feet] in depth, and the stones of which they were composed, more than sixty feet in length, while the superstructure contained, of the whitest marble, stones nearly sixty-eight feet long, more than seven feet high, and nine broad. The circuit of the whole building was four furlongs; its height one hundred cubits [150 feet]; one hundred and sixty pillars, each twenty-seven feet high, ornamented and sustained the immense and ponderous edifice. In the front, spacious and lofty galleries, wainscoted with cedar, were supported by columns of white marble, in uniform rows. In short, says Josephus, nothing could surpass even the exterior of this temple, for its elegant and curious workmanship. It was adorned with solid plates of gold that rivaled the beauty of the rising sun, and were scarcely less dazzling to the eye than the beams of that luminary. Of those parts of the building which were not gilt; when viewed from a distance, some, says he, appeared like pillars of snow, and some, like *mountains of white marble.* The splendor of the interior parts of the temple corresponded with its external magnificence. It was decorated and enriched by everything that was costly, elegant, and superb. Religious donations and offerings had poured into this wonderful repository of precious stores from every part of the world, during many successive ages.

In the lower temple were placed those sacred curiosities, the seven branched candlestick of pure gold, the table for the showbread, and the altar of incense; the two latter of which were covered with plates of the same metal. In the sanctuary were several doors fifty-five cubits [83 feet] high and sixteen [24 feet] in breadth which were all likewise of gold. Before these doors hung a veil of the most beautiful Babylonian tapestry, composed of scarlet, blue, and purple, exquisitely interwoven, and wrought up to the highest degree of art. From the top of the ceiling depended branches and leaves of vines, and large clusters of grapes, hanging down five or six feet, all of gold and of most admirable workmanship. In addition to these proofs of the splendor and riches of the temple, may be noticed its eastern gate of pure Corinthian brass more esteemed even than the precious metals — the golden folding doors of the chambers — the beautiful carved work, gilding, and painting of the galleries — golden vessels of the sanctuary — the sacerdotal vestments of scarlet, violet, and purple — the vast wealth of the treasury — abundance of precious stones, and immense quantities of all kinds of costly spices and perfumes. In short, the most valuable and sumptuous of whatever nature, or art, or opulence could supply was enclosed within the consecrated walls of this magnificent and venerable edifice.

So much concerning this celebrated city, and its still more celebrated temple. We shall now consider our LORD's *prophecies* relating to their destruction.

Jesus' Prophecies Concerning the Destruction of Jerusalem

On the second day of the week, immediately preceding His crucifixion, our blessed Savior made His public and triumphal entry into Jerusalem amidst the acclamations of a very great multitude of His disciples, who hailed Him KING OF ZION; and with palm-branches, the emblems of victory, in their hands, rejoiced and gave praises to God for all the mighty works they had seen, singing "Hosanna! Blessed be the King that cometh in the name of the LORD! Peace in heaven, and glory in the highest!" But while the people thus exulted, and triumphantly congratulated the Messiah, He struggling with the deepest emotions of pity and compassion for Jerusalem, beheld the city and wept over it, saying,

> "If you had known, even you, at least in this day, the things that belong to your peace! But now they are hidden from your eyes; for the days shall come upon you, that your enemies shall cast a trench about you, and surround you, and keep you in on every side; And shall lay you even with the ground, and your children within you, and they shall not leave in you one stone upon another; *because you knew not the time of your visitation.*"[2]

On the fourth day of that week, being only two days before His death, He went for the last time into the temple to teach the people. While He was thus employed, the High

---

[2] Luke 19:42-44.

Priests and the Elders, the Herodians, the Sadducees, and Pharisees, successively came to Him, questioning him with subtlety, being desirous to "entangle him in his talk," to whom, with His accustomed dignity and wisdom, He returned answers which carried conviction to their hearts, and at once silenced and astonished them. Then, turning to His disciples, and the whole multitude, He addressed to them a discourse of very uncommon energy, in which, with most exquisite keenness of reproof, He exposed and condemned the cruelty and pride, the hypocrisy and sensuality of the Pharisees and Scribes.

Having next foretold the barbarous treatment which His Apostles would receive at their hands, He proceeded to denounce against Jerusalem the dire and heavy vengeance that had for ages been accumulating in the vials of divine displeasure, expressly declaring that it should be poured out upon the *then-existing generation,* adding the inimitably tender and pathetic apostrophe to this devoted city:

> "O Jerusalem, Jerusalem, you that kill the prophets, and stone them who are sent to you, how often would I have gathered your children together, even as a hen gathers her chickens under her wings, and you would not! Behold! Your **house** is left to you desolate; for I say to you, you shall not see me henceforth, till you shall say, *Blessed is he that comes in the name of the Lord!*"[3]

Having said this, He went out of the temple, and, as He departed, His disciples drew His attention to the wonderful

---

[3] Matthew 23:37-39.

magnitude and splendor of the edifice. They spoke of "how
it was adorned with goodly stones and gifts;" and said to
Him, "Master *see what manner of stones and buildings are
here!*" And Jesus said to them, "Do you not see all these
things? Truly I say to you, there shall not be left here one
stone upon another that shall not be thrown down."

When we consider the antiquity and sanctity of the
temple, its stupendous fabric, its solidity, and the uncommon
magnitude of the stones of which it was composed, we may,
in some measure, conceive of the amazement which this
declaration of our LORD must have excited in the mind of
His disciples. Nevertheless, this remarkable prediction, as
we shall see in the sequel, was literally fulfilled, and as our
LORD had foretold, it came to pass even during the existence of the generation to which He addressed it.

Our Lord now retired to the Mount of Olives, to which
place the disciples followed Him, in order to make more
particular inquiries relative to the time when the calamitous
events, foretold by Him, would come to pass. We have already intimated that the Mount of Olives commanded a full
view of Jerusalem and the temple. No situation, therefore,
could have been better adapted to give energy to a prediction
which related chiefly to their total ruin and demolition; *and*
if we suppose (and the supposition is highly probable) that
our LORD, while in the act of speaking, pointed to the ma-
jestic and stupendous edifices, whose destruction He foretold—every word which He then uttered must have been
clothed with inexpressible sublimity, and derived from the
circumstances of the surrounding scenery, a force and effect
which it is not possible adequately to conceive.

"Tell us, when shall these things be? and what shall be the sign when all these things shall be fulfilled?" Such were the questions of the disciples, in answer to which our LORD condescended to give them a particular account of the several important events that would precede it, as well as of the prognostics which would announce the approaching desolations. He additionally includes suitable directions for the regulation of their conduct under the various trials to which they were to be exposed. He commences with a caution: "Take heed," says He, "that no man deceive you; for many shall come in my name, saying, I am Christ, and shall deceive many."

The False Christs

The necessity for this friendly warning soon appeared; for within one year after our Lord's ascension, rose Dositheus the Samaritan, who had the boldness to assert that he was the Messiah, of whom Moses prophesied; while his disciple Simon Magus deluded *multitudes* into a belief that he, himself, was the "GREAT POWER OF GOD."

About three years afterwards another Samaritan impostor appeared, and declared that he would show the people the sacred utensils, said to have been deposited by Moses, in Mount Gerizim. Induced by an idea that the Messiah, their great deliverer, was now come, an armed multitude assembled under him, but Pilate speedily defeated them, and slew their chief. While Cuspius Fadus was procurator in Judea, another deceiver arose, whose name was Theudas. [4] This man actually succeeded so far as to persuade a *very great multitude* to take their effects and follow him to Jordan,

---

[4] This is not the Theudas mentioned in Acts 5:36.

assuring them that the river would divide at his command. Fadus, however, pursued them with a troop of horses, and slew many of them, and the impostor's head was cut off and carried to Jerusalem.

Under the government of Felix, deceivers rose up daily in Judea, and persuaded the people to follow them into the wilderness, assuring them that they should there behold conspicuous signs and wonders performed by the AL-MIGHTY. Of these Felix, from time to time, apprehended many and put them to death.

About this period (A.D. 55) arose another Felix, the celebrated Egyptian impostor, who collected *thirty-thousand followers,* and persuaded them to accompany him to the Mount of Olives, telling, them that from thence they should see the walls of Jerusalem fall down at his command, as a prelude to the capture of the Roman garrison, and to their obtaining the sovereignty of the city. The Roman governor, however, interpreting this to be the beginning of revolt, immediately attacked them, slew four hundred of them, and dispersed the rest; but the Egyptian escaped.

In the time of Porcius Festus (A.D. 60) another distinguished impostor seduced the people by promising them deliverance from the Roman yoke if they would follow him into *the wilderness;* but Festus sent out an armed force which speedily destroyed both the deceiver and his followers.

In short, impostors to a divine commission, continually and fatally deceived the people, and at once justified the caution, and fulfilled the prediction of our LORD.

If it be objected that none of these impostors, except Dositheus, assumed the name of *Messiah,* we reply that the groveling expectations of the Jews was directed to a Messiah who should merely deliver them from the Roman yoke, and "restore the kingdom to Jerusalem;" and such were the pretensions of these deceivers. This expectation, indeed, is the only true solution of these strange and reputed insurrections; which will naturally remind the reader of the following prophetic expressions of our LORD: "I am come in my Father's name, and ye receive me not; if another shall come *in his own name,* him ye will receive." "If they shall say unto you, 'Behold he is in the *desert!'* go not forth." "They will show[5] (or pretend to show) great *signs and wonders,"* etc.

Our Savior thus proceeded: "And ye shall hear of wars, and rumors of wars; see that ye be not troubled: for all these things must come to pass, but the end is not yet, *for nation shall rise up against nation and kingdom against kingdom,* and great earthquakes shall be in *divers places,* and *famines,* and *pestilences:* all these are the *beginnings of sorrows.*"[6]

"Wars and rumors of wars..."

Luke 21:11, *"Wars and rumors of wars."* These commotions, like distant thunder, that forebodes the approaching storm,

> "At first heard solemn o'er the *verge* of heaven,"

were so frequent from the death of our Lord until the destruction of Jerusalem, that whole interval might, with propriety, be appealed to in illustration of this prophecy. One hundred and fifty of the copious pages of Josephus, which

---

[5] The original word signifies that, in Scripture language, there is a clear distinction betwixt giving a sign and the sign itself. This is sufficiently proved by Deuteronomy 13:1-2

[6] Matthew 24:7-8

contain the history of this period, are everywhere stained with blood. To particularize in a few instances: About three years after the death of Christ, a war broke out between Herod and Aretas, king of Arabia Petraea, in which the army of the former was cut off. This was *kingdom rising against kingdom.* Wars are usually preceded by rumors. It may, therefore, appear absurd to attempt a distinct elucidation of this part of the prophecy; nevertheless, it ought not to be omitted, that about this time, the emperor Caligula, having ordered his statue to be placed in the temple of Jerusalem, and the Jews having persisted to refuse him, the whole nation were so much alarmed by the mere apprehension of war, that they neglected even to till their lands! The storm, however, blew over.

About this period a great number of Jews, on account of a pestilence which raged at Babylon, removed from that city to Seleucia, where the Greeks and Syrians rose against them and destroyed of this devoted people more than *five myriads!* "The extent of this slaughter (says Josephus) had no parallel in any former period of their history." Again, about five years after this dreadful massacre, there happened a severe contest between the Jews at Perea, and the Philadelphians, respecting the limits of a city called Mia, in which many of the former were slain. This was nation rising up against nation. Four years afterwards, under Cumanus, an indignity was offered to the Jews within the precincts of the temple, by a Roman soldier, which they violently resented; but, upon the approach of the Romans in great force, their terror was so excessive, and so disorderly and precipitate was their flight, that not less than *ten thousand* Jews were trodden to death in the streets. This, again, was nation rising up against nation. Four years more had not elapsed before the Jews made war against the Samaritans, and ravaged their country. The people of Samaria had murdered a Galilean, who was going up to Jerusalem to keep the Passover, and the Jews thus revenged it. At Caesarea, the Jews having had a sharp contention with the Syrians for the government of the city, an appeal was made to Rome, who decreed it to the Syrians. This event laid the foundation of a most cruel and sanguinary contest between the *two nations.* The Jews, mortified by disappointment, and inflamed by jealousy, rose against the Syrians, who successfully repelled them. In the city of Caesarea alone upwards of *twenty thousand Jews* were slain.

The flame, however, was not now quenched; it spread its destructive rage wherever the Jew and Syrians dwelt together in the same place: throughout every city, town, and village, mutual animosity and slaughter prevailed. At Damascus, Tyre, Ascalon, Gadara, and Scythopolis, the carnage was dreadful. At the first of these cities, *ten thousand Jews* were slain in one hour, and at Scythopolis *thirteen, thousand* treacherously in one night. At Alexandria the Jews, aggrieved by the oppressions of the Romans, rose against them; but the Romans, gaining the ascendancy, slew of that nation *fifty thousand persons,* sparing neither infants nor the aged. And after this, at the siege of Jopata, not less than *forty thousand* Jews perished. While these destructive contests prevailed in the East, the western parts of the Roman Empire were rent by the fierce contentious of Galba, Otho, and Vertellis; of which three emperors, it is remarkable that they all, together with Nero, their immediate predecessor, died a violent death within the short space of eighteen months. Finally, the whole nation of the Jews took up arms against the Romans, king Agrippa, etc. and provoked that dreadful war which, in a few years, deluged Judea in blood, and laid its capital in ruins.

If it be here objected that, because wars occur so frequently, it would be improper to attribute to supernatural foresight a successful prediction respecting them, it is replied that much of this objection will be removed by considering the incompetency of even statesmen themselves to foretell the condition, only for a few years, of the very nation whose affairs they administer. It is a well-known fact that the present minister of Great Britain, on the very eve of the late long and destructive war with the French Republic, held out to this country a picture of fifteen successive years of peace. Indeed, the nice points on which peace and war often depend baffle all calculations from present aspects; and a rumor of *war,* so loud and so alarming, as even to suspend the operations of husbandry, might terminate, as we have just seen, in *nothing but rumor.* Farther, let it be considered, that the wars to which this part of our LORD's prophecy referred were to be of two kinds, and that the event corresponded accordingly; that they occurred within the period to which He had assigned them; that they fell with the most destructive severity on the Jews, to whom the prophecy at large chiefly related, and that the person who predicted them was not in the condition of a *statesman,* but in that of *a Carpenter's son!* On this subject more in another place.

"And great earthquakes shall be in diverse places."

Of these significant emblems of political commotions, several occurred within the scene of this prophecy, and, as our Savior predicted, in *diverse places.* In the reign of Claudius there was one at Rome, and another at Apamea in Syria, where many of the Jews resided. The *earthquake* at the latter place was so destructive, that the emperor, in order to relieve the distresses of the inhabitants, suspended taxing them for five years. Both these *earthquakes* are recorded by Tacitus. There was also one during the same reign in Crete. This is mentioned by Philostratus, in his Life of Apollonius, who says, that "there were others at Smyrna, Miletus, Chios, and Samos; in all which places *Jews* had settled."

In the reign of Nero there was an *earthquake* at Laodicea. Tacitus records this also. It is likewise mentioned by Eusebius and Orosius, who add that Hierapolis and Colossae, as well as Laodicea, were overthrown by an *earthquake.* There was also one in Campania in this reign (of this both Tacitus and Seneca speak), and another at Rome in the reign of Galba, recorded by Suetonius; to all which may be added those which happened on that dreadful night when the Idumeans were excluded from Jerusalem, a short time before the siege commenced. "A heavy storm (says Josephus) burst on them during the night; violent winds arose, accompanied with the most excessive rains, with constant lightnings, most tremendous thunderings, and with dreadful roarings of *earthquakes.* It seemed as if the system of the world had been confounded for the destruction of mankind; and one might well conjecture that these were signs of no common events."

"Famines"

Our *LORD* predicted *"famines"* also. Of these the principal was that which Agabus foretold would happen in the days of Claudius, as related in the Acts of the Apostles. It begun in the fourth year of his reign, and was of long continuance. It extended through Greece, and even into Italy, but was felt most severely in Judea, and especially at Jerusalem, where many perished for want of bread. This famine is recorded by Josephus also, who relates that "an assaron of corn was sold for five drachmae" (i e. about 3½ pints for $350)[7]. It is likewise noticed by Eusebius and Orosius. To alleviate this terrible calamity, Helena, queen of Adiabena, who was at that time in Jerusalem, ordered large supplies of grain to be sent from Alexandria; and Izates, her son, consigned vast sums to the governors of Jerusalem, to be applied to the relief of the more indigent sufferers. The Gentile Christian converts residing in foreign countries also sent, at the insistence of St. Paul, liberal contributions, to relieve the distresses of their Jewish brethren.[8] Dion Cassius relates that there was likewise a *famine* in the first year of Claudius which prevailed at Rome, and in other parts of Italy; and, in the *eleventh* year of the same emperor, there was another, mentioned by Eusebius. To these may be added those that afflicted the inhabitants of several of the cities of Galilee and Judea, which were besieged and taken, previous to the siege of Jerusalem, where the climax of national misery, arising from this and every other cause, was so awfully completed.

"Pestilences"

Our Lord adds *"pestilences"* likewise. Pestilence treads upon the heels of famine, it may therefore reasonably be presumed, that this terrible scourge accompanied the fam-

---

[7] This is the 2018 equivalent.—Editor.
[8] 1 Corinthians 16:3

ines which have just been enumerated. History, however, particularly distinguishes two instances of this calamity, which occurred before the commencement of the Jewish war. The first took place at Babylon about A.D. 40, and raged so alarmingly, that great *multitudes of Jews* fled from that city to Seleucia for safety, as has been hinted at already. The other happened at Rome A.D. 65, and carried off prodigious *multitudes.* Both Tacitus and Suetonius also record that similar calamities prevailed during this period, in various parts of the Roman Empire. After *Jerusalem* was surrounded by the army of Titus, *pestilential* diseases soon made their appearance there to aggravate the miseries and deepen the horrors of the siege. They were partly occasioned by the immense multitudes which were crowded together in the city, partly by the putrid effluvia which arose from the unburied dead, and partly from spread of *famine.*

"Signs...from heaven"

Our Lord proceeded, "And fearful sights and great *signs* shall there be from *heaven."[9]* Josephus has collected the chief of these portents together, and introduces his account by a reflection on the strange infatuation, which could induce his countrymen to give heed to impostors and unfounded reports, while disregarding the divine admonitions, confirmed (as he asserts they were) by the following extraordinary *signs*:

1. "A meteor, resembling a sword,[10] hung over Jerusalem during one whole year." This could not be a comet, for it was stationary and was visible for twelve successive

---

[9] Luke 21:11
[10] Compare with 1 Chronicles 21:16.

29

months. A sword too, though a fit emblem for destruction, but ill represents a *comet*.

2. "On the eighth of the month Zanthicus (before the feast of unleavened bread), at the ninth hour of the night, there shone round about the altar, and the circumjacent buildings of the temple, a light equal to the brightness of the day, which continued for the space of half an hour." This could not be the effect of lightning, nor of a vivid aurora borealis, for it was confined to a particular spot and the light shone *without variation for thirty minutes.*

3. "As the High Priests were leading a heifer to the altar to be sacrificed, she brought forth [gave birth to] a *lamb,* in the midst of the temple." Such is the strange account given by the historian. Some may regard it as a "Grecian fable," while others may think that they discern in this prodigy a miraculous rebuke of Jewish infidelity and impiety, for rejecting the ANTITYPICAL Lamb, who had offered up Himself as an atonement, "once *for all,"* and who, by thus completely fulfilling their design, had virtually abrogated the Levitical sacrifices. However this may be, the circumstances of the prodigy are remarkable. It did not occur in an obscure part of the city, but in the *temple*; not at an ordinary time, but at *the Passover,* the season of our LORD'S crucifixion; in the presence, not of the common priests merely, but of the *High* Priests and their attendants, and that while they were *leading the sacrifice to the altar.*

4. "About the sixth hour of the night, the eastern gate of the temple was seen to open without human assistance." When the guards informed the Curator of this event, he sent men to assist them in shutting it, who with great difficulty succeeded. — This gate, as has been observed already, 'Was

of solid brass, and required twenty men to close it every evening. It could not have been opened by a "strong gust of wind," or a *slight* earthquake;" for Josephus says, it was secured by iron bolts and bars, which were let down into a large threshold; consisting of one entire stone."[11]

5. "Soon after the feast of the Passover, in various parts of the country, before the setting of the sun, chariots and armed men were seen in the air, passing round about Jerusalem." Neither could this portentous spectacle be occasioned by the *aurora borealis,* for it occurred *before the setting of the sun.* Nor could it be merely the fancy of a few villagers, gazing at the heavens, for it was seen in *various parts* of the country.

6. "At the subsequent feast of Pentecost, while the priests were going by night into the inner temple to perform their customary ministrations, they first felt, as they said, a shaking, accompanied by an indistinct murmuring, and afterwards voices as of a multitude, saying, in a distinct and earnest manner, "LET US DEPART HENCE." This gradation will remind the reader of that awful transaction, which the feast of Pentecost was principally instituted to commemorate. First, a shaking was heard; this would naturally induce the priests to listen. Then, an unintelligible murmur follows; this would more powerfully arrest their attention. And while it was thus awakened and fixed, they heard, says Josephus, the voices as of a multitude, *distinctly* pronouncing the words "LET US DEPART HENCE." — And accordingly, before the period for celebrating this feast returned, the Jewish war had commenced, and in the space of

---

[11] The conclusion which the Jews drew from this event was that the security of the temple was gone.

three years afterwards, Jerusalem was surrounded by the Roman army, the temple converted into a citadel, and its sacred courts streaming with the blood of *human* victims.

7. As the last and most fearful omen, Josephus relates that one Jesus, the son of Ananus, a rustic of the lower class, during the Feast of Tabernacles suddenly exclaimed in the temple, "A voice from the east a voice from the west — a voice from the four winds — a voice against Jerusalem and the temple — a voice against bridegrooms and brides — a voice against the whole people!" These words he incessantly proclaimed aloud both day and night, through all the streets of Jerusalem, for seven years and five months together, commencing at a time (A.D. 62) when the city was in a state of peace, and overflowing with prosperity, and terminating amidst the horrors of the siege. This disturber, having excited the attention of the magistracy, was brought before Albinus the Roman governor, who commanded that he should be *scourged*. But the severest stripes drew from him neither tears nor supplications. As he never thanked those who relieved, so neither did he complain of the injustice of those who struck him. And no other answer could the governor obtain to his interrogatories, but his usual denunciation of "Woe, woe to Jerusalem!" which he still continued to proclaim through the city, but especially during the festivals, when his manner became more earnest, and the tone of his voice louder. At length, on the commencement of the siege, he ascended the walls, and, in a more powerful voice than ever, exclaimed, "Woe, woe to this city, this temple, and this people!" And then, with a presentment of his own death, added, "Woe, woe to myself!" He had scarcely uttered these

words when a stone from one of the Roman engines killed him on the spot.

Such are the prodigies related by Josephus, and which, excepting the first, he places in the year immediately preceding the Jewish war. Several of them are recorded also by Tacitus. Nevertheless, it ought to be observed, that they are received by Christian writers cautiously, and with various degrees of credit. Those Christians, however, who are most skeptical, and who resolve them into natural causes, admit the "superintendence of GOD to awaken his people by some of these means." Whatever the facts may be, it is clear that they correspond to our LORD'S prediction of *"fearful sights, and great signs from heaven;"* and ought to be deemed a sufficient answer to the objector, who demands whether any such appearances are respectably recorded.

Persecutions

The next prediction of our LORD related to the persecutions of His disciples: "They shall lay their hands on you, and persecute you, delivering you up to the synagogues and into prisons, *being brought before kings and rulers* for my name's sake."[12] "[A]nd they shall deliver you up to councils, and in the synagogues ye shall be beaten,"[13] "and some of you shall they *cause to be put to death*."[14]

In the very infancy of the Christian church, these unmerited and unprovoked cruelties began to be inflicted. — Our LORD, and His forerunner John the Baptist, had already been put to death; the Apostles Peter and John were first

---

[12] Luke 21:12
[13] Mark 13:9
[14] Luke 21:16

imprisoned, and then, together with the other Apostles, were scourged before the Jewish council. Stephen, after confounding the *Sanhedrim* with his irresistible eloquence, was *stoned to death;* Herod Agrippa "stretched forth his hands to vex certain of the church," *beheaded* James the brother of John, and again *imprisoned* Peter, designing to put him to death also.

St. Paul *pleaded* before the Jewish council at Jerusalem, and *before Felix the Roman governor,* who trembled on the judgment seat, while the intrepid prisoner "reasoned of righteousness, temperance, and judgment to come!" Two years afterwards he was brought *before the tribunal of Festus* (who had succeeded Felix in the government), king Agrippa the younger being present, who, while the governor scoffed, ingenuously acknowledged the force of the Apostle's eloquence, and, half convinced, exclaimed, "Almost thou persuadest *me* to be a Christian." Lastly, he pleaded before the *emperor Nero* at Rome; he was also brought with Silas *before the rulers* at Philippi, where both of them were *scourg*ed and *imprisoned.* Paul was likewise imprisoned two years in Judea, and afterwards twice at Rome, each time for the space of two years. He was *scourged* by the Jews five times, thrice *beaten* with rods, and once stoned; nay, he himself, before his conversion, was an instrument of fulfilling the predictions. St. Luke relates of him that "he made havoc of the church, entering into every house, and *arresting* men and women, committed them to *prison* — when they were *put to death* he gave his voice against them; he punished them often in every *synagogue,* and, *persecuted* them even into strange cities — and to this agree his own declarations.[15]

At length, about two years before the Jewish war, the first general persecution commenced at the instigation of the emperor Nero, "who," says Tacitus, "inflicted upon the Christians punishments exquisitely painful." Multitudes suffered a cruel martyrdom amidst derision and insults, and included in that number are the venerable Apostles St. Peter and St. Paul.

"hated of all nations..."

Our LORD continues, "And ye shall be hated of *all nations* for my *name's sake*."[16] The hatred from which the above-recited persecutions sprang was not provoked on the part of the Christians by a rebellious resistance to established authority, or by any violations of law, but was the unavoidable consequence of their sustaining the *name,* and imitating the character of their Master. "It was a war," says Tertullian, "against the very name: to be a *Christian* was of itself crime enough." And to the same effect, Pliny in his letter to Trajan says: "I asked them whether they were Christians; if they confessed it, I asked them a second and a third time, threatening them with punishment; and those who persevered I commanded to be led away to death." — It is added, "of all nations." Whatever animosity or dissensions might exsist between the Gentiles and the Jews on other points, they were at all times ready to unite and cooperate in the persecution of the humble followers of Him, who came to be a *light* to the former, and the *glory* of the latter.

---

[15] Acts 26:10-11; Galatians 1:23
[16] Matthew 24:9

"shall betray one another."

"And then shall many be offended, and shall betray one another."[17] Concerning this fact, the following decisive testimony of Tacitus may suffice: speaking of the persecutions of the Christians under Nero, to which we have just alluded, he adds "several were seized, who confessed, and by their discovery a great multitude of others were convicted and barbarously executed."

"Gospel...shall be preached in all the world"

"And this Gospel of the kingdom shall be preached in all the world, for a witness unto all nations, and then shall the end (i.e. of the Jewish dispensation) come."[18] Of the fulfillment of this prediction, the Epistles of St. Paul, addressed to the Christians at Rome, Corinth, Galatia, Ephesus, Philippi, Colosse, Thessalonica; and those of Peter to such as resided in Pontus, Cappadocia, and Bithynia, are monuments now standing — for neither of these Apostles were living when the Jewish war commenced. St. Paul, too, in his Epistle to the Romans, informs them that "their faith was spoken of throughout the world; and in that to the Colossians he observes that the "Gospel had been preached to every creature under heaven." Clement, who was a fellow-laborer with the Apostle, relates of him that "he taught the whole world righteousness, travelling from the East westward to the borders of the ocean." Eusebius says that "the Apostles preached the Gospel in all the world, and that some of them

---

[17] Matthew 24:10
[18] Matthew 24:14

passed beyond the bounds of the ocean, and visited the Britannic isles."[19] So says *Theodoret* also.

"It appears," says Bishop Newton, "from the writers of the history of the church, that before the destruction of Jerusalem the Gospel was not only preached in the *Lesser Asia,* and *Greece,* and *Italy*, the great theatres of action then in the world, but was likewise propagated as far northward as *Scythia*, as far southward as *Ethiopia,* as far eastward as *Parthia* and *India*, as far westward as *Spain* and *Britain*." And Tacitus asserts that "the Christian religion, which arose in Judea, spread over many parts of the world, and extended to Rome itself, where the professors of it, as early as the time of Nero, amounted to a vast multitude," insomuch that their numbers excited the jealousy of the government.

Thus completely was fulfilled a prediction contrary to every conclusion that could have been grounded on human probability, and to the accomplishment of which every kind of impediment was incessantly opposed. The reputed Son of a mechanic instructs a few simple fishermen in a *new dispensation* destitute of worldly incentives, but full of self-denials, sacrifices, and sufferings, and tells them that in about forty years it should spread over all the world. It spreads accordingly; and, in defiance of the exasperated bigotry of the Jews, and of all the authority, power, and active opposition of the Gentiles, is established, within that period, in all the countries into which it penetrates. Can anyone doubt but that the prediction and its fulfillment were equally divine?

---

[19] It is admitted that the phrase "to all the world," "every creature," etc. are hyperbolical; but then, taken in their connection, they evidently import the *universality of the preaching and spread* of the Gospel, *previously to the destruction of Jerusalem,* which is the point to be *proved.*

Such, briefly, is the account that history gives of the several events and signs, which our Lord had foretold would precede the destruction of the Holy City. No sooner were His predictions accomplished, than a most unaccountable infatuation seized upon the whole Jewish nation; so that they not only provoked, but seemed even to rush into the midst of those unparalleled calamities, which at length totally over-whelmed them. In an essay of this sort it is impossible to enter into a minute detail of the origin and progress of these evils; but such particulars as illustrate the fulfillment of the remaining part of the prophecy, and justify the strong language in which it is couched, shall be presented to the reader.

The Destruction of Jerusalem

From the conquest of their country by Pompey, about sixty years B.C. the Jews had, on several occasions, manifested a refractory spirit; but after Judas the Gaulonite and Sadduc the Pharisee had taught them, that submission to the Roman assessments would pave the way to a state of abject slavery, this temper displayed itself with increasing malignity and violence. Rebellious tumults and insurrections became fame and more frequent and alarming; and to these the mercenary exactions of Florus, the Roman governor, not a little contributed. At length Eleazer, son of the High Priest, persuaded those who officiated in the temple to reject the sacrifices of foreigners, and no longer to offer up prayers for them. Thus an insult was thrown upon Caesar, his sacrifice rejected, and the foundation of the Roman war laid. The disturbances among the Jews still continuing, Cestius Gallus, president of Syria, marched an army into Judea, in order to quell them, and his career was everywhere marked with blood and desolation. As he proceeded, he plundered and burnt the beautiful city of Zabulon, Joppa, and all the villages which lay in his way. At Joppa he slew of the inhabitants *eight thousand four hundred*. He laid waste the district of Narbatene, and, sending an army into Galilee, slew there *two thousand* of the seditious Jews. He then burnt the city of Lydda; and after having repulsed the Jews, who made a desperate sally upon him, encamped, at length, at the distance of about one mile from Jerusalem, On the fourth day be entered its gate and burnt three divisions of the city, and might now, by its capture, have put a period to the war; but through the treacherous persuasions of his officers, instead of pursuing his advantages, he most unaccountably raised the siege, and fled from the city with the utmost precipitation. The Jews, however, pursued him as far as Antipatris, and, with little loss to themselves, slew of his army nearly six thousand men. After this disaster had befallen Cestius, the more opulent of the Jews (says Josephus) forsook Jerusalem as men do a sinking ship. And it is with reason supposed, that on this occasion many of the Christians, or converted Jews, who dwelt there, recollecting the warnings or their divine Master, retired to Pella, a place beyond Jordan, situated in a *mountainous* country,[20] whither (according to Eusebius, who resided near the spot) they came from Jerusalem, and settled, before the war (under Vespasian) began.

Other providential opportunities for escaping afterwards occurred, of which, it is probable, those who were now left behind availed themselves; for it is a striking act, and such as cannot be contemplated by the pious mind without sentiments of devout admiration, that history does not record that even one CHRISTIAN perished in the siege of Jerusalem. Enduring to the end faithful to their blessed MASTER, they, gave credit to his predictions, and escaped the calamity. Thus were fulfilled the words of our Lord, Matthew 24:13. "He that shall endure unto the end (i. e. of the scene of this prophecy) shall be saved," 1: e. from the calamities which will involve all those who shall continue obstinate in unbelief.

Nero, having been informed of the defeat of Cestius, immediately appointed Vespasian, a man of tried valor, to

---

[20] Such was our Lord's admonition. . .: "Let them which be in Judea flee *into the mountains,"* &c. *Matthew 16:1-28; Matthew 22:1-46.*

prosecute the war against the Jews, who, assisted by his son Titus, soon collected at Ptolemais an. army of *sixty thousand* men. From hence, in the spring of 67 A.D. he marched into Judea, everywhere spreading the most cruel havoc and devastation; the Roman soldiers, on various occasions, sparing neither infants nor the aged. For fifteen months Vespasian proceeded in this sanguinary career, during which period he reduced all the strong towns of Galilee, and the chief of those in Judea, destroying at least one **hundred and fifty thousand** *of* the inhabitants Among the terrible calamities which at this time happened to the Jews, those which befell them at Joppa, which had been rebuilt, deserve particular notice. Their frequent piracies bad provoked the vengeance of Vespasian. The Jews fled before his army to their ships; but a tempest immediately arose, and pursued such as stood out to sea, and overset them, while the rest were dashed vessel against vessel, and against the rocks, in the most tremendous manner. In this *perplexity* many were drowned, some were crushed by the broken ships, others killed themselves, and such as reached the shore were slain by the merciless Romans. The sea for a long space was stained with blood; *four thousand two hundred* dead bodies were strewed along the coast, and, dreadful to relate, not an individual survived to report this great calamity at Jerusalem. Such events were foretold by our LORD, when he said, "There shall be distress of nations, with *perplexity; the sea and the waves roaring.* " Luke 21:25.

Vespasian, after proceeding as far as Jericho, returned to Caesarea, in order to make preparation for his grand attempt against Jerusalem. While he was thus employed, he received intelligence of the death of Nero; whereupon, not knowing what the will of the future emperor might be, he prudently resolved to suspend, for the present, the execution of his design. Thus the Almighty gave the Jews a second respite, which continued nearly *two* years; but *they* repented not of their crimes, neither were they in the least degree reclaimed, but rather proceeded to acts of still greater enormity.

The flame of civil dissension again burst out and with more dreadful fury. In the heart of Jerusalem two factions contended for the sovereignty, and raged against each other with rancorous and destructive animosity. A division of one of these factions having been excluded from the city (vide page 26,) forcibly entered it during the night. Athirst for blood, and inflamed by revenge, they spared neither age, sex, nor infancy; and the morning beheld *eight thousand five hundred* dead bodies lying in the streets of the holy city. They plundered every house, and having found the chief priests Anaius and Jesus, not only slew them, but, insulting their bodies, cast them forth unburied. They slaughtered the common people as unfeelingly as if they had been a herd of the vilest beasts. The nobles they first imprisoned, then scourged, and when they could not by these means attach them to their party, they bestowed death upon them as a favor. Of the higher classes *twelve thousand* perished in this manner; nor did anyone dare to shed a tear, or utter a groan, openly, through fear of a similar fate. Death, indeed, was the penalty of the lightest and heaviest accusations, nor did any escape through the meanness of their birth, or their poverty. Such as fled were intercepted and slain: their carcasses lay in heaps on all the public roads: every symptom of pity seemed utterly extinguished, and with it, all respect for authority, both human and divine.

While Jerusalem was a prey to these ferocious and devouring factions, every part of Judea was scourged and laid waste by bands of robbers and murderers, who plundered the towns; and, in case of resistance, slew the inhabitants, not sparing either women or children. Simon, son of Gioras, the commander of one of these bands, at the head of forty thousand banditti, having with some difficulty entered Jerusalem, gave birth to a third faction, and the flame of civil discord blazed out again, with still more destructive fury. The three factions, rendered frantic by drunkenness, rage, and desperation, trampling on heaps of slain, fought against each other with brutal savageness and madness. Even such as brought sacrifices to the temple were murdered. The dead bodies of priests and worshippers, both natives and foreigners were heaped together, and a lake of blood stagnated in the sacred courts. John of Gischala, who headed one of the factions, burnt storehouses full of provisions; and Simon, his great antagonist, who headed another of them, soon afterwards followed his example. Thus they cut the very sinews of their own strength.

At this critical and alarming conjuncture, intelligence arrived that the Roman an army was approaching the city. The Jews were petrified with astonishment and fear; there was no time for counsel, no hope of pacification, no means of flight: — all was wild disorder and perplexity: — nothing was to be heard but "the confused noise of the warrior," — nothing to be seen but garments rolled in blood," — nothing to be expected from the Romans but signal and exemplary vengeance. A ceaseless cry of combatants was heard day and night, and yet the lamentations of mourners were still more dreadful. The consternation and terror which now prevailed induced many inhabitants to desire that a foreign foe might come, and effect their deliverance. Such was the horrible condition of the place when Titus and his army presented themselves, and encamped before Jerusalem; but, alas! not to deliver it from its miseries but to fulfill the prediction, and vindicate the benevolent warning of our Lord: "When *ye* see (he had said to his disciples) the *abomination of desolation,* spoken or by the prophet Daniel, standing in the holy place,[21] and Jerusalem surrounded by armies (or camps,) then let those who are in the midst of Jerusalem depart, and let not those who are in the country enter into her," for " then know that the desolation thereof *is nigh.* " Matthew 24:15; Matthew 24:21; Luke 21:20; Luke 21:1-11.

These armies, we do not hesitate to affirm were those of the Romans, who now invested the city. From the time of the Babylonian captivity, idolatry had been held as an *abomination* by the Jews. This national aversion was manifested even against the images of their gods and emperors, which the Roman armies carried in their standards; so that, in a time of peace, Pilate, and afterwards Vitellius, at the request of some eminent Jews, on this account avoided marching their forces through Judea. Of the *desolating* disposition which now governed the Roman army, the history of the Jewish war, and especially of the final demolition of the holy city, presents an awful and signal example. Jerusalem was not captured merely, but, with its celebrated temple, laid in ruins. Lest, however, the army of Titus should not be sufficiently designated by this expression, our LORD adds,

---

[21] Not only was the temple and the mountain on which it stood accounted holy, but also the whole city of Jerusalem, and several furlongs of land round about it. Neh. 11:1-36 : I, Isa. 53:1-12 : I; Dan. 9:24; and Matthew 27:53.

"Wheresoever the carcass is, there will the *eagles* be gathered together." Matthew 24:28. The Jewish state, indeed, at this time, was fitly compared to a carcass. The sceptre of Judah, 1:e. its civil and political authority, the life of its religion, and the glory of its temple, were departed. It was, in short, morally and judicially *dead.* The eagle, whose ruling instinct is rapine and murder, as fitly represented the fierce and sanguinary temper of the Romans, and, perhaps, might be intended to refer also to the principal figure on their ensigns, which, however obnoxious to the Jews, were at length planted in the midst of the holy city, and finally on the

temple itself.

The day on which Titus encompassed Jerusalem, was the feast of the Passover; and it is deserving of the very particular attention of the reader, that this was the anniversary of that memorable period in which the Jews crucified their Messiah! At this season multitudes came up from all the surrounding country, and from distant parts, to keep the festival. How suitable and how kind, then, was the prophetic admonition of our LORD, and how clearly he into futurity when he said "Let not them that are in the countries enter into Jerusalem." Luke 21:21.

Nevertheless, the city was at this time crowded with Jewish strangers, and foreigners from all parts, so that the whole nation may be considered as having been shut up in one prison, preparatory to the execution of the Divine vengeance; and, according to Josephus this event took place *suddenly;* thus, not only fulfilling the predictions of our LORD, that these calamities should come, like the swift-darting lightning "that cometh out of the east and shineth even unto the West," and "as a *snare* on all of them (the Jews) who dwelt upon the face of the whole earth" (Matthew 24:27, and Luke 21:35,) but justifying, also, his friendly direction, that those who fled from the place should use the utmost possible expedition.

On the appearance of the Roman army, the factious Jews united, and, rushing furiously out of the city repulsed the *tenth legion,* which was with difficulty preserved. This event caused a short suspension of hostilities, and, by opening the gates, gave an opportunity to such as were so disposed to make their escape; which before this they could not have attempted without interruption, from the suspicion that they wished to revolt to the Romans. This success inspired the Jews with confidence, and they resolved to defend their city to the very uttermost; but it did not prevent the renewal of their civil broils. The faction under Eleazer having dispersed, and arranged themselves under the two other leaders John and Simon, there ensued a scene of the most dreadful contention, plunder, and conflagration: the middle space of the city being burnt, and the wretched inhabitants made the prize of the contending parties. The Romans at length gained possession of two of the three walls which defended the city, and fear once more united the factions. This pause, to their fury had, however, scarcely begun when famine made its ghastly appearance in the Jewish army. It had for some time been silently approaching, and many of the peaceful and the poor had already perished for want of necessaries.

With this new calamity, strange to relate, the madness of the factions again returned, and the city presented a new picture of' wretchedness. Impelled by the cravings of hunger, they snatched the staff of life out of each other's hands, and many devoured the grain unprepared. Tortures were inflicted for the discovery of a handful of meal; women forced food from their husbands, and children from their fathers, and even mothers from their infants, and while sucking children were wasting away in their arms, they scrupled not to take away the vital drops which sustained them! So justly did our LORD pronounce a woe on "them that should give suck in those days." (Matthew 24:19.)

This dreadful scourge at length drove multitudes of the Jews out of the city into the enemy's camp, where the Romans crucified them in such numbers, that, as Josephus relates, space was wanted for the crosses, and crosses for the captives; and it having been discovered that some of them had swallowed gold, the Arabs and Syrians, who were incorporated in the Roman army, impelled by avarice, with unexampled cruelty ripped open two thousand of the deserters in one night. Titus, touched by these calamities, in person entreated the Jews to surrender, but they answered him with revilings. Exasperated by their obstinacy and insolence, he now resolved to surround the city by a circumvallation, (a trench of 39 furlongs in circuit and strengthened with 13 towers,) which with astonishing activity was effected by the soldiers in three days. Thus was fulfilled another of our LORD 's predictions, for he had said, while addressing this devoted city, "Thine enemies shall cast a trench about thee, and compass thee round about, and keep thee in on every side." Luke 19:43.

As no supplies whatever could now enter the walls, the famine rapidly extended itself, and, increasing in horror, devoured whole families. The tops of houses, and the recesses of the city, were covered with the carcasses of women, children, and aged men. The young men appeared like spectres in the places of public resort, and fell down lifeless in the streets. The dead were too numerous to be interred, and many expired in the performance of this office. — The public calamity was too great for lamentation. Silence, and, as it were, a black and deadly night, overspread the city. — But even such a scene could not awe the robbers; they spoiled the tombs, and stripped the dead of their grave-clothes, with an unfeeling and wild laughter. They tried the edges of their swords on their carcasses, and even on some that were yet breathing; while Simon Goras chose this melancholy and awful period to manifest the deep malignity and cruelty of his nature in the execution of the High Priest Matthias, and his three sons, whom he caused to be condemned as favorers of the Romans. The father, in consideration of his having opened the city gates to Simon, begged that he might be executed previously to his children; but the unfeeling tyrant gave orders that he should be dispatched in the last place, and in his expiring moments insultingly asked him, whether the Romans could then relieve him.

While the city was in this dismal situation, a Jew named Mannaeus fled to Titus, and informed him, that from the beginning of the siege (4th mo. 14th) to the 1st of 7th mo. following, *one hundred and fifteen thousand eight hundred and eighty* dead bodies had been carried through one gate only, which he had guarded. This man had been appointed to pay the public allowance for carrying the bodies out, and was therefore obliged to register them. Soon after, several respectable individuals deserted to the Romans, and assured Titus that the whole number of the poor who had been cast out at the different gates was not less than *six hundred thousand*. The report of these calamities excited pity in the Romans, and in a particular manner affected Titus, who, while surveying the immense number of dead bodies which were piled up under the walls, raised his hands towards Heaven, and, appealing to the Almighty, solemnly protested that he had not been the cause of these deplorable calamities; which, indeed, the Jews, by their unexampled wickedness rebellion, and obstinacy, had brought down upon their own heads.

After this, Josephus, in the name of Titus, earnestly exhorted John and his adherents to surrender; but the insolent rebel returned nothing but reproaches and imprecations, declaring his firm persuasion that Jerusalem, as it was GOD'S own city, could never be taken: thus literally fulfilling the declaration of Micah, that the Jews, in their extremity, notwithstanding their crimes, would presumptuously "lean upon the LORD, and say, 'Is not the LORD among us? none evil can come upon us." (Mic. 3:11)

Meanwhile the horrors of famine grew still more melancholy and afflictive. The Jews, for of food were at length compelled to eat their belts, their sandals, the skins of their shields, dried grass, and even the ordure of oxen. In the depth or this horrible extremity, a Jewess of noble family urged by the intolerable cravings of hunger, slew her infant child, and prepared it for a meal; and had actually eaten one half thereof, when the soldiers, allured by tile smell of food, threatened her with instant death if she refused to discover it. 'Intimidated by this menace, she immediately produced the remains of her son, which petrified them with horror. At the recital of this melancholy and affecting occurrence, the whole city stood aghast, and poured forth their congratulations on those whom death had hurried away from such heartrending scenes. Indeed, humanity at once shudders and sickens at the narration, nor can any one of the least sensibility reflect upon the pitiable condition to which the female part of the inhabitants of Jerusalem must at this time have been reduced, without experiencing the tenderest emotions of sympathy, or refrain from tears while he reads our SAVIOR'S pathetic address to the women who "bewailed him" as he was led to Calvary, wherein he evidently refers to these very calamities: "Daughters of Jerusalem, weep not for me, but for yourselves and for your children; for, behold, the days are coming in which they shall say, 'Blessed are the barren, and the wombs that never bare, and the breasts that never gave suck. " Luke 23:29.

The above melancholy fact was also literally foretold by Moses: "The *tender and delicate women* among you (said he, addressing Israel) who would not adventure to set the sole of her foot upon the ground for delicateness and tenderness, her eye shall be evil. . . toward *her young one. . .* which she shall bear," and *"eat for want of* all *things, secretly, in the* siege and *straitness* wherewith, thine enemy shall distress thee in thy gates. " (Deut. 28:56-57.) This prediction was partially fulfilled, when Samaria the capital of the revolted tribes, was, besieged by Benhadad; and afterwards at Jerusalem, previously to its capture by Nebuchadnezzar; but its exact and literal accomplishment in relation to a lady of rank, delicately and voluptuously educated, was reserved for the period of which we are now speaking. And it deserves particular regard, as a circumstance which very greatly enhances the importance of this prophecy, that the history of the world does not record that a parallel instance of unnatural barbarity ever occurred during the siege of any other place, in any other age or nation whatsoever. Indeed, Josephus himself declares that, if there had not been many credible witnesses of the fact, he would not have recorded it, "because," as he remarks, "such a shocking, violation of nature never having been perpetuated by any Greek or barbarian," the insertion of it might have diminished the credibility of his history.

While famine continued thus to spread its destructive rage through the city, the Romans, after many ineffectual attempts, at length succeeded in demolishing part of the inner wall, possessed themselves of the great tower of Antonia, and advanced towards the Temple, which Titus, in a council of war had determined to preserve as an ornament to the empire, and as a monument of his success; but the Almighty had determined otherwise; for now, in the revolution of ages, was arrived that fatal day, (the 10th of 8th mo.) emphatically called " a day of vengeance," (Luke 21:21.) on which the Temple had formerly been destroyed by the king of Babylon. A Roman soldier, urged, as he declared, by a divine impulse, regardless of the command of Titus climbed on the shoulders of another, and threw a flaming brand into the golden window of the Temple, which instantly set the building on fire. The Jews, anxious above all things to save that sacred edifice, in which they superstitiously trusted for security, with a *dreadful outcry,* rushed in to extinguish the flames. Titus also, being informed of the conflagration, hastened to the spot in his chariot, attended by his principal officers and legions; but in vain he waved his hand and raised his voice, commanding his soldiers to extinguish the fire; so great was the uproar and confusion, that no attention was paid even to him. The Romans, willfully deaf instead of extinguishing the flames, spread them wider and wider.

Actuated by the fiercest impulses: rancor and revenge against the Jews, they rushed furiously upon them, slaying some with the sword, trampling others under their feet, or crushing them to death against the walls. Many, falling amongst the smoking ruins of the porches and galleries, were suffocated. The unarmed poor, and even sick persons, were slaughtered without mercy. Of these unhappy people numbers were left weltering in their gore. Multitudes of the dead and dying were heaped round about the altar, to which they had formerly fled for protection, while the steps that led from it into the outer court were literally deluged with their blood.

Finding it impossible to restrain the impetuosity and cruelty of his soldiers, the Commander in chief proceeded, with some of his superior officers, to take a survey of those parts of the edifice which were still uninjured by the conflagration. It had not, at this time, reached the *inner* Temple, which Titus entered, and viewed with silent admiration. Struck with the magnificence of its architecture, and the beauty of its decorations, which even surpassed the report of fame concerning them; and perceiving that the sanctuary had not yet caught fire, he redoubled his efforts to stop the progress of the flames. He condescended even to entreat his soldiers to exert all their strength and activity for this purpose, and appointed a centurion of the guards to punish them if they again disregarded him: but all was in vain. The delirious rage of the soldiery knew no bounds. Eager for plunder and for slaughter, they alike contemned the solicitations and menaces of their General. Even while he was thus intent upon the preservation of the sanctuary, one of the soldiers was actually employed in setting fire to the doorposts, which caused the conflagration to become general. Titus and his officers were now compelled to retire, and none remained to check the fury of the soldiers or the flames. The Romans, exasperated to the highest pitch against the Jews, seized every person whom they could find, and, without the least regard to sex, age or quality, first plundered and then slew them. The old and the young, the common people and the priests, those who surrendered and those who resisted, were equally involved in this horrible and indiscriminate carnage.

Meanwhile the Temple continued burning, until at length, vast as was its size, the flames completely enveloped the whole building; which, from the extent of the conflagration, impressed the distant spectator with an idea that the whole city was now on fire. The tumult and disorder which ensued upon this event, it is impossible (says Josephus) for language to describe. The Roman legions made the most horrid outcries; the rebels, finding themselves exposed to the fury of both fire and sword, screamed dreadfully; while the unhappy people who were pent up between the enemy and the flames, deplored their situation in the most pitiable complaints. Those on the hill and those in the city seemed mutually to return the groans of each other. Such as were expiring through famine, were revived by this hideous scene, and seemed to acquire new spirits to deplore their misfortunes. The lamentations from the city wore re-echoed from the adjacent mountains, and places beyond Jordan. The flames which enveloped the Temple were so violent and impetuous, that the lofty hill on which it stood appeared, even front its deep foundations, as one large body of fire. The blood of the sufferers flowed in proportion to the rage of this destructive element; and the number of the slain exceeded all calculation. The ground could not be seen for the dead bodies, over which the Romans trampled in pursuit of the fugitives; while the crackling noise of the devouring flames mingled with the clamor of arms, the groans of the dying and the shrieks of despair, augmented the tremendous horror of a scene, to which the pages of history can furnish no parallel.

Amongst the tragic events which at this time occurred, the following is more particularly deserving of notice: a false prophet, pretending to a divine commission, affirmed that, if the people would repair to the Temple, they should behold signs of their speedy deliverance. Accordingly about *six thousand* persons, chiefly women and children, assembled in a gallery that was yet standing, on the outside of the building. Whilst they waited in anxious expectation of the promised miracle, the Romans with the most wanton barbarity, set fire to the gallery; from which, multitudes; rendered frantic by their horrible situation, precipitated themselves on the ruins below, and were killed by the fall: while, awful to relate, the rest, without a single exception, perished in the flames. So necessary was our *Lord's second* premonition not to give credit to "false prophets," who should pretend "to show great signs and wonders." In this last caution, as the connection of the prophecy demonstrates, he evidently refers to the period of the siege, but in the former to the interval immediately preceding the Jewish war. (Matthew 24:1-51 : Compare 5, and 23, 24, 25, 26, verses.)

The Temple now presented little more than a heap of ruins; and the Roman army as in triumph on the event, came and reared their ensigns against a fragment of the eastern gate, and, with sacrifices of thanksgiving, proclaimed the imperial majesty of Titus, with every possible demonstration of joy.

Thus terminated the glory and existence of this sacred and venerable Edifice, which from its stupendous size, its massy solidity, and astonishing strength, seemed formed to resist the most violent operations of human force, and to stand, like the pyramids, amid the shocks of successive ages, until the final dissolution of the globe.[22]

For five days after the destruction of the Temple, the priests who had escaped, sat, pining with hunger, on the top of one of its broken walls; at length, they came down, and humbly asked the pardon of Titus, which, however, he refused to grant them, saying, that, "as the Temple, for the sake of which he would have spared them, was destroyed, it was but fit that its priests should perish also;" whereupon he commanded that they should be put to death.

The leaders of the factions being now pressed on all sides, begged a conference with Titus, who offered to spare their lives, provided that they would lay down their arms. With this reasonable condition, however, they refused to comply; upon which Titus, exasperated by their obstinacy, resolved, that he would hereafter grant, no pardon to the

---

[22] From its first foundation by king Solomon, until its destruction tinder Vespasian, were one thousand and thirty years, seven months, and fifteen days; and from its re-erection by Haggai, to the same period, six hundred and thirty-nine years and forty five days. It has been already hinted, that, by a very singular coincidence, it was now reduced to ashes in the same month, and on the same day of the month, on which it had formerly been burnt by the Babylonians. These two eras are distinguished also by another extraordinary coincidence, which Josephus, in one of [its addresses to the Jews, pointed out to them as one of the signs which foreboded the destruction of their city.

"The fountains," said he, "flow copiously for Titus, which to you were dried up; for, before he came, you know that both Siloam failed, and all the springs without the city, so that water was bought by the amphora [a vessel containing about seven gallons;] but now they are so abundant to your enemies, as to suffice, not only for themselves and their cattle, but also for their gardens. This wonder you also formerly experienced when, the king of Babylonians laid siege to your city."

insurgents, and ordered a proclamation to be made to this effect. The Romans had now full license to ravage and destroy. Early the following morning they set fire to the castle, the register-office, the council-chamber, and the palace of the queen Helena; and then spread themselves throughout the city, slaughtering wherever they came, and burning the dead bodies which were scattered over every street, and on the floors of almost every house. In the royal palace, where immense treasures were deposited, the seditious Jews murdered *eight thousand four hundred* of their own nation, and afterwards plundered their property. Prodigious numbers of deserters, also, who escaped from the tyrants, and fled into enemy's camp, were slain. The soldiers, however, at length, weary of killing, and satiated with the blood which they had spilt, laid down their swords and sought to gratify avarice. For this purpose they took the Jews, together with their wives and families, and publicly sold them, like cattle in a market, but at a very low price; for *multitudes* were exposed to sale, while the purchasers were few in number. And now were fulfilled the words of' Moses: "And ye shall be sold for bond-men and bond-women, and no man shall buy you." (Deut. 28:68.)

The Romans having become masters of the *lower* city, set it on fire. The Jews now fled to the *higher,* from whence, their pride and insolence yet unabated, they continued to exasperate their enemies and even appeared to view the burning of the town below them with tokens of pleasure. In a short time, however, the walls of the higher city were demolished by the Roman engines and the Jews, lately so-haughty and presumptuous, now trembling and panic-struck, fell on their faces, and deplored their own infatuation. Such as were in the towers, deemed impregnable to human force, beyond measure affrighted, strangely forsook them, and sought refuge in caverns and subterraneous passages; in which dismal retreats no less than *two thousand* dead bodies were afterwards found. Thus, as our Lord had predicted, did these miserable creatures, in effect, say "to the mountains, 'Fall on us;' and to the rocks, ' Cover us. " (Luke 23:20.)

The walls of the city being now completely in possession of the Romans, they hoisted their colors upon the towers, and burst forth into the most triumphant acclamations. After this, all annoyance from the Jews being at an end, the soldiers gave an unbridled license to their fury against the inhabitants. They first plundered, and then set fire to the houses. They ranged through the streets with drawn swords in their hands, murdering every Jew whom they met, without distinction; till at length, the bodies of the dead choked up all the alleys and narrow passes while their blood literally flowed down the channels of the city in streams. As it drew towards evening, the soldiers exchanged the sword for the torch, and, amidst the darkness of this awful night, set fire to the remaining divisions of the place. The vial of divine wrath, which had been so long pouring out upon this devoted city was now emptying, and JERUSALEM, once "a praise in all the earth," and the subject of a thousand prophecies, deprived of the staff of life, wrapped in flames, and bleeding on every side sunk into utter ruin and desolation. This memorable siege terminated on the eighth day of the ninth month, A.D. 70: its duration was nearly five months, the Romans having invested the city on the fourteenth day of the fourth month, preceding.

Before their final demolition, however, Titus took a survey of the city and its fortifications; and, while contemplating their impregnable strength, could not help ascribing his success to the peculiar interposition of the ALMIGHTY HIMSELF. "Had not God himself (exclaimed he) aided out operations, and driven the Jews from their fortresses, it would have been absolutely impossible to have taken them; for what could men, and the force of engines, have done against such towers as these?" After this he commanded that the city should be razed to its foundations, excepting only the three lofty towers Hippocos, Phasael, and Mariamne, which he suffered to remain as evidences of its strength, and as trophies of his victory. There was left standing, also, a small part of the western wall; as a rampart for a garrison, to keep the surrounding country in subjection. Titus now gave orders that those Jews only who resisted should be slain; but the soldiers, equally void of pity and remorse, slew even the sick and the aged. The robbers and seditious were all punished with death: the tallest and most beautiful youths, together with several of the Jewish nobles were reserved by Titus to grace his triumphal entry into Rome. After this selection, all above the age of seventeen were sent in chains into Egypt, to be employed there as slaves, or distributed throughout the empire to be sacrificed as gladiators in the amphitheatres; whilst those who were under this age, were exposed to sale.

During the time that these things were transacted, *eleven thousand* Jews, guarded by one of the generals, named Fronto, were literally starved to death. This melancholy occurrence happened partly through the scarcity of provisions, and partly through their own obstinacy, and the negligence of the Romans.

Of the Jews destroyed during the siege, Josephus reckons not less than *ONE MILLION AND ONE HUNDRED THOUSAND*, to which must be added, above *TWO-HUNDRED AND THIRTY-SEVEN THOUSAND* who perished in other places, and *innumerable multitudes* who were swept away by famine, and pestilence, and of which no calculation could be made. Not less than *two thousand* laid violent hands upon themselves. Of the captives the whole was about *NINETY-SEVEN THOUSAND*. Of the Two great leaders of the Jews, who had both been made prisoners, John was doomed to a dungeon for life; while Simon, together with John, in triumph at Rome was scourged, and put to death as a malefactor.

In executing the command of Titus, relative to the demolition of Jerusalem, the Roman soldiers not only threw down the buildings, but even dug up their foundations, and so completely leveled the whole circuit of the city, that a stranger would scarcely have known that it had ever been inhabited by human beings. Thus was this great City, which only five *months* before, had been crowded with nearly *two millions* of people, who gloried in its impregnable strength, entirely depopulated, and leveled with the ground. And thus, also was our LORD'S prediction, that her enemies should "lay her *even with the ground,*" and "should not leave in her *one stone upon another," (Luke 19:44*.) most strikingly and fully accomplished! — This fact is confirmed by Eusebius, who asserts that he himself saw the city lying in ruins; and Josephus introduces Eleazer as exclaiming "Where is our great city, which, it was believed, GOD inhabited? It is altogether *rooted and torn up from its foundations;* and the only monument of it that remains, is the camp of its destroyers pitched amidst its reliques!"

Concerning the Temple, our LORD had foretold, particularly, that, notwithstanding their wonderful dimensions, there should "not be left one stone upon another that should not be thrown down;" and, accordingly, it is recorded, in the Talmud, and by Maimonides, that Terentius Rufus, captain of the army of Titus, absolutely *ploughed* up the foundations of the Temple with a ploughshare. Now, also, was literally fulfilled that prophecy of Micah- "Therefore shall Zion, for your sakes (i.e. for your wickedness,) be *ploughed as a field,* and Jerusalem shall become heaps, and the mountain of the LORD's house as the high places of the forest." (Mic. 3:12)

Thus awfully complete and ever, beyond example, were the calamities which befell the Jewish nation, and especially the city of Jerusalem. With what truth, then, did our LORD declare, that there should "be great tribulation, *such as was not since the beginning of the world,* no, nor ever shall be!" (Matthew 24:21.) Such was the prediction: the language in which Josephus declares its *fulfillment is* an exact counterpart to it: "If the misfortunes," says he," of all nations, from *the beginning of the world,* were compared with those which befell the Jews, they would appear far less in comparison;" and again, *"No other city ever suffered such things,* as no other generation, from the *beginning of the world, was* ever more fruitful in wickedness." These were, indeed, "the days of vengeance," that all things which are written (especially by Moses, Joel, and Daniel,) might be fulfilled." Luke 21:22. Nor were the calamities of this ill-fated nation even now ended; for there were still other places to subdue; and our

LORD had thus predicted, "*wheresoever the* carcass is, *there will* the *eagles be gathered together.* " (Matthew 24:28.) After the destruction of Jerusalem **seventeen hundred** Jews who surrendered at Macherus were slain, and of fugitives not less than **three thousand** in the wood of Jardes. Titus having marched his army to Caesarea, he there, with great splendor, celebrated the birthday of his brother Domitian; and according to the barbarous manner of those times, punished many Jews in honor of it. The number who were burnt, and who fell by fighting with wild beasts, and in mutual combats, exceeded **two thousand five hundred.**

At the siege of Massada, Eleazer, the commander, instigated the garrison to burn their stores, and to destroy first the women and children, and then themselves. Dreadful as it is to relate, this horrid design was executed. They were in number **nine hundred and sixty**. Ten were chosen to perform the bloody work: the rest sat 'on the ground,' and embracing their wives and children stretched out their necks to the sword: one was afterwards appointed to destroy the remaining nine, and then himself. The survivor, when he had looked round to see that all were slain, set fire to the place, and plugged his sword into his own bosom. Nevertheless less, two women and five children successfully concealed themselves, and witnessed the whole transaction. When the Romans advanced to the attack in the morning, one of the women gave them a distinct account of this melancholy affair, and struck them with amazement at the contempt of death which had been displayed by the Jews. After this event, if we except the transitory insurrection of the Sicarii, under Jonathan, all opposition on the part of the Jews everywhere ceased. It was the submission of impotence and despair. The peace that ensued was the effect of the direst necessity. The rich territory of Judea was converted into a desolate *waste*. Everywhere ruin and desolation presented itself to the solitary passenger, and a melancholy and death-like silence reigned over the whole region.

The mournful and desolate condition of Judea, at this time, is exactly described by the prophet Isaiah, in the following of his prophecy: "The cities were without inhabitant, and the houses without a man, and the land was utterly desolate, and the LORD had removed men far away, and there was a great forsaking in the midst of the land." (Isa. 6:11-12.)

The Catastrophe which has now been reviewed, cannot but be deemed one of the most extraordinary that has happened since the foundation of the world; and as it has pleased the Almighty to make it the subject of a very large proportion of the prophecies both of the Jewish and Christian Scriptures, so he has ordained that the particular events which accomplished them should be recorded, with very remarkable precision, and by a man most singularly preserved,[23] qualified, and circumstanced for this purpose. But with respect to this latter point, he shall speak for himself: "At first," says Josephus, "I fought against the Romans, but was afterwards forced to be present in the Roman camp. At the time I surrendered, Vespasian and Titus kept me in bonds, but obliged me to attend them continually. Afterwards I was set at liberty, and accompanied Titus when he came from Alexandria to the siege of Jerusalem. During *this time nothing was done that escaped my knowledge*. What happened in the Roman camp I saw, and wrote *down care-*

---

[23] Three times his life was preserved as by a miracle.

fully. As to the information the deserters brought out of the city, I was the only man that understood it. Afterwards I got leisure at Rome; and when all my materials were prepared, I procured the help of one to assist me in writing Greek. — Thus I composed the history of those transactions, and I appealed both to Titus and Vespasian for the truth of it; to which also Julius Archelaus, Herod, and King Agrippa, bore their testimony."

All remark here is needless; but it should not be forgotten, that Josephus was a Jew, obstinately attached to his religion; and that, although he has circumstantially related every remarkable event of that period, he seems studiously to have avoided such as had any reference to *JESUS CHRIST,* whose history, and even the genuineness of this is disputed, he sums up in about twelve lines. No one, therefore, can reasonably entertain a suspicion, that the service he has rendered to Christianity, by his narrative of the transactions of the Jewish war, was at all the effect of design. The fidelity of Josephus, as an historian, is, indeed, universally admitted; and Scaliger even affirms, that, not only in the affairs of the Jews, but in those of foreign nations also, he deserves more credit than all the Greek and Roman writers put together.

Nor is the peculiar character of Titus, the chief commander in this war, unworthy of our particular regard. Vespasian, his father, had risen out of obscurity and was elected emperor, contrary to his avowed inclination, about the commencement of the conflict; and thus the chief command devolved upon Titus, the most unlikely man throughout the Roman armies to become a scourge to Jerusalem. He was eminently distinguished for his great tenderness and humanity, which he displayed in a variety of instances during the siege. He repeatedly made pacific overtures to the Jews, and deeply lamented the infatuation that rejected them. In short, he did everything which a military commander could do, to spare them, and to preserve their city and temple, but without effect. Thus was the will of God accomplished by the agency, although contrary to the wish, of Titus; and his predicted interposition, to punish his rebellious and apostate people, in this way rendered more conspicuously evident.

The State of the Jews since AD 70

The history of the Jews, subsequently to the time of Josephus, still further corroborates the truth of our *SAVIOR'S* prophecies concerning that oppressed and persecuted people. Into this inquiry, however, the limits of the present essay will not allow us to enter particularly. Our LORD foretold, generally, that they should "fall by the edge of the-sword, and be led away captive into all nations; and that Jerusalem should be trodden down of the Gentiles, until the times of the Gentiles should be fulfilled" (Luke 21:24.) and these predictions may be regarded as a faithful epitome of the circumstances of the Jews and also of their city, from the period in which it was delivered, down even to our own times.

In order to demonstrate the accomplishment of these predictions, we appeal, therefore, to universal history, and to every country under heaven.

"In the reign of Adrian," say Bishop Newton, "*nine hundred and eighty-five of* their best towns were sacked and demolished, *five hundred and eighty thousand* men fell by the sword, in battle, besides an infinite multitude who perished by, famine, and sickness, and fire; so that Judea was depopulated, and an almost incredible number of every age and of each sex, were sold like horses and dispersed over the face of the earth-" (Newton, vol. I, page 18:) The war which gave rise to these calamities happened about forty-four years after the destruction of Jerusalem; during which time the Jews had greatly multiplied in Judea. About fifty years after the latter event, Ælius Adrian built a new city on Mount Calvary, and called it Ælia, after his own name; but no *Jew*

68

was suffered to come near it. He placed in it a heathen colony, and erected a temple to Jupiter Capitolinus, on the ruins of the temple of JEHOVAH. — This event contributed greatly to provoke the sanguinary war to which we have just alluded. The Jews afterwards burnt the new city; which Adrian, however, rebuilt, and re-established the colony. In contempt of the Jews, he ordered a marble statue of a sow to be placed over its principal gate, and prohibited them entering the city under pain of death, and forbad them even to look at it from a distance. He also ordered fairs to be held annually for the sale of captive Jews, and *banished* such as dwelt in Canaan into Egypt. Constantine greatly improved the city, and restored to it the name of Jerusalem, but still he did not permit the Jews to dwell there. To punish an attempt to recover the possession of their capital, he ordered their ears to be cut off, their bodies to be marked as rebels, and dispersed them through all the provinces of the empire as vagabonds and slaves.

Jovian having revived the severe edicts of Adrian, which Julian had suspended, the wretched Jews even bribed the soldiers with money, for the privilege only of beholding the sacred ruins of their city and temple, and weeping over them, which they were peculiarly solicitous to do on the anniversary of that memorable day, on which they were taken and destroyed by the Romans. In short, during every successive age and in all nations, this ill-fated people have been constantly persecuted, enslaved, contemned, harassed, and oppressed; banished from one country to another, and abused in all; while countless multitudes have, at different periods, been barbarously massacred, particularly in Persia, Syria,

Palestine, and Egypt; and in Germany, Hungary, France, and Spain.

The undisputed facts are, that Jerusalem has not since been in possession of the Jews, but has been successively occupied by the Romans, Arabic Saracens, Franks, Mamalucs, and lastly by the Turks, who now possess it. It has never regained its former distinction and prosperity. It has always been *trodden down*. The *eagles* of idolatrous Rome, the *crescent of* Mahomet, and the *banner of* Popery, have by turns been displayed amidst the ruins of the sanctuary; and a Mahomedan mosque, to the extent of a mile in circumference, now covers the spot where the Temple formerly stood. — The territory of Judea, then one of the most fertile countries on the globe, has for more than *seventeen hundred years* continued a desolate waste. The Jews themselves, still miraculously preserved a distinct people, are, as we see, scattered over the whole earth, invigorating the faith of the Christian, flashing conviction in the face of the infidel, and constituting an universal, permanent, and invincible evidence of the truth of Christianity.

In order to invalidate this evidence, the apostate emperor Julian, impelled by a spirit of enmity against the Christians, about A.D. 363, made an attempt to rebuild the city and temple of Jerusalem, and to recall the Jews to their own country. He assigned immense sums for the execution of this great design, and commanded Alypius or Antioch (who had formerly served as a lieutenant in Britain) to superintend the work, and the governor of the province to assist him therein. But (says Ammianus Marcelianus) "whilst they urged with vigor and diligence the execution of the work, horrible balls of fire, breaking out near the foundation, with frequent and reiterated attacks, rendered the place, from time to time, inaccessible to the scorched and blasted workmen; and the victorious element continuing in this manner obstinately and resolutely bent, as it were, to drive them to a distance, the undertaking was abandoned." Speaking of this event, even Gibbon, who is notorious for his skepticism, acknowledges, that "an earthquake, a whirlwind, and a fiery eruption, which overturned and scattered the new foundations of the Temple, are attested, with some variations, by contemporary and respectable evidence, by Ambrose bishop of Milan, Chrysostom, and Gregory Nazianzen, the latter of whom published his account before the expiration of the same year."[24] To these may be added the names of Zemuch David, a Jew (who confesses that "Julian was hindered by GOD in the attempt,") of Ruffinus a Latin, of Theodoret and Sozomen among the orthodox, of Philostorgius an Arian, and of Socrates a favorer of the Novatians, who all recorded the same wonderful interposition of Providence, *while the eye-witness of the fact were yet living.* The words of Sozomen to this purport are remarkable: "If it seem yet incredible (says he) to any one, he may repair both to witnesses of it yet living, and to them who have heard it from their mouths; yea, they may view the foundations, lying yet bare and naked. Besides, it may be added, that no other reason has ever been alleged why Julian should abandon his magnificent but impious design.

Thus was this celebrated Emperor "taken in his own craftiness," and his presumptuous attempt to frustrate the plans, and falsify the declarations of infinite Omnipotence

---

[24] Decline and Fall, vol. 4, Sec. page 107.

and Wisdom, converted into a new and striking evidence of their certainty and truth.

Objections Answered

We shall now proceed to reply to two or three objections which may be rashly opposed to the impregnable argument which the preceding account furnishes in defense of our religion.

I. It may be alleged, that the prophecies, whose fulfillment has been demonstrated, were not written until after the events, to which they refer, were past.

Assertion is not proof; and even a conjecture to this effect, in the face of the historic testimony, and general sentiment of seventeen ages, would be ridiculous. On the faith, then, of all antiquity, we affirm, that the books in the Scriptures, containing these predictions were written before the destruction of Jerusalem, and we confirm this assertion by particular proof. The book of St. Matthew, who *died previously* to *that event, supposed* to have been written about eight years after the ascension of our Savior, was *published* before the dispersion of the Apostles; for Eusebius says, that St. Bartholemew took a copy Of it with him to *India;* and the dispersion of the Apostles took place within twelve years after the ascension of our Lord. St. Mark must have written his book at the latest in the time of Nero, for he died in the eighth year of that emperor's reign. The book by St. Luke was written before the Acts, as the first verses of that narrative prove; and the Acts were written before the death of Paul, for they carry down his history only to A.D. 63; whereas he was not crucified until the 12th of Nero, the very year before the Jewish war commenced. Of Luke's death the time is uncertain. As to the Evangelist John, he both lived and wrote after the destruction of Jerusalem; "but then, as if purposely to prevent this very cavil, his book does not record the prophecies which foretold it! Learned men, indeed, differ with regard to the *precise* year in which the Evangelists Matthew, Mark, and Luke wrote their respective books; but they universally agree, that they were both written and published *before* the destruction of Jerusalem. As to the book by St. John, some are of opinion that it was written *before, and* some *after* that event.

II. If it be objected, that, although the narratives might be written and published before the destruction of Jerusalem, yet that the predictions relating to that event may be subsequent interpolations; we reply, that this cannot but be considered as a preposterous supposition, because those predictions are not confined to the particular chapters to which we have referred, but are closely and inseparably interwoven with the general texture of the history — because the character of the style is uniform — because there is no allusion, in conformity to the practice of the sacred historians, to the fulfillment of these prophecies (particularly, Acts 11:28.) — because such an attempt must have destroyed the cause it professed to serve, and lastly, because "no unbeliever of the primitive times, whether Jew or Gentile, when pressed, as both frequently were, by this prophecy, appear to have had recourse to the charge of forgery or interpolation." It may be added also, that, in modern times, no distinguished unbeliever (not even the arch infidels Voltaire and Gibbon) has had the temerity so much as to insinuate a charge of this nature.

III. It may be alleged, that the accomplishment of our Lord's predictions relative to the destruction of Jerusalem, ought not to be deemed supernatural, inasmuch as the distresses of all great cities, during a siege, are similar, and because it is probable that, *sometime or other,* such should be the fate of every city of this description; and that since the obstinacy of the Jews was great, and their fortifications strong, *when war did come,* Jerusalem was more likely to suffer under that form of it than any other.

In answer to this objection, we remark, that it was not merely foretold that Jerusalem was to be destroyed, but that it was to be destroyed by the *Romans:* and so it was. But was this *then* a *likely* event? When our LORD delivered his predictions, Judea was already completely in their hands. Was it a *probable* thing that it should be desolated by its own masters? Or was it a *natural* thing that they should be in-different to the revenue which was derived from a country so Populous and so fertile? Again, was it *likely* that this petty province should provoke the wrath and defy the power of the universal empire? Or was it to be supposed that the mistress of the world, irresistible to all nations, instead of controlling, should deem it worthy of her *utterly to exterminate* a state comparatively so insignificant? Or did it accord with the disposition or custom of the Romans, like Goth to demolish buildings famed for their antiquity and magnificence? Ra-ther was it not to have been expected that they would pre-serve them, to maintain the renown and glory of their em-pire? Nevertheless, as we have seen, they *did* destroy them, and even the illustrious Temple of Jerusalem, the chief or-nament of Asia, and the wonder of the world. But it was predicted that "thus it must be;" and *therefore* Titus himself with all his authority and exertions, could *not* preserve it.

IV. If this prophecy be ascribed to political sagacity, we would ask, on the supposition of the infidel, how it happened that a *Carpenter's Son,* living nearly the whole of his life in privacy, associating chiefly with the poor, without access to the councils of princes, or to the society of the great should possess a degree of political discernment to which no *Statesman* would deem less than folly to lay claim? Besides, how came he to predict the ruin of his *own country,* and at that very reason, too, when all his countrymen turned their eyes to a Deliverer, who should *restore sovereignty, consolidate its power, and extend both its boundaries and its renown?* And lastly, how came he even to conceive, much more cherish, such an idea, diametrically contrary as it was to all his stubborn and deep rooted prejudices *as a Jew?*

Thus we perceive that the very objections which infidelity opposes to our argument, instead of invalidating tend only more fully to illustrate and confirm it.

Conclusion

Let us, then, if we are Christians *indeed* offer up our grateful acknowledgments to the ALMIGHTY, who has laid such a firm foundation for our faith. Let us exult in the inviolable certainty of the Holy Word, viz. CHRIST, (John 1:1-51 :) and assure ourselves that his *promises* are as infallible as his *predictions:* To "the witness" within us (1 John 5:10.) and to an acquaintance with the interior excellence of the gospel, let us labor to add a more perfect knowledge of the historical and moral evidence which defends it; that thus we may be better qualified to convince gainsayers.

If we are *Christians* in *name only,* let us receive a salutary admonition from that exemplary vengeance which was inflicted by the ALMIGHTY upon the whole Jewish nation; who, while "they *professed* that they *knew God,* in *works* denied him;" and while they boasted that they were his peculiar people, remained "strangers to the covenant of promise." Let us also seriously reflect, that as he was not a *Jew* who was only one "outwardly," "in the letter" merely, and whose praise was of men — so now, in like manner, he only is a *Christian* who is one " inwardly," whose religion is seated in the heart; "in the spirit and not in the letter"; whose praise is not of men, but of God." (Rom. 2:28-29.)

Let the *Unbeliever,* or the *professed Deist,* for whose benefit, chiefly, the preceding pages were written, seriously ponder their contents. It may be proper to state, that the faith which we wish him to possess is not merely an admission upon evidence, that " all Scripture is given by inspiration of God," (which, standing alone, has no higher value than the faith of education,) but a VITAL, ACTIVE PRINCIPLE, A FAITH that will purify the heart;" that "works by love that will enable him to " fight the good FIGHT," " to overcome the world," and to obtain "a crown of life," and an "in corruptible inheritance" in heaven.